THE "C" FLIGHT LINE BOOK

The Author at 22 Air School

THE "C" FLIGHT LINE BOOK

Tony Hobson

A Square One Publication

First published in 1995 by
Square One Publications
The Tudor House,
16 Church Street
Upton on Severn, Worcs WR8 0HT

British Library Cataloguing in Publication Data
is available for this book

ISBN 1 899955 03 8

Typeset in Palatino 10pt by Avon Dataset, Bidford on Avon
Printed by Biddles Ltd, Guildford, England

To Captain Tony Lawrenson, SAAF
who started the whole thing . . .

and with thanks to
my fellow flying instructor
Group Captain Freddie Sledmere. AFC,
who helped recall it

TONY HOBSON

CONTENTS

A Cast of Characters

FOREWORD

by

Air Marshal Sir Ivor Broom, KCB, CBE, DSO, DFC, AFC

Extracts from a line book of 50 years ago will bring back amusing memories to the countless thousands who have had the privilege of learning to fly – but the uninitiated might well ask 'What is a line?'. Let it be said immediately that a 'line' in aviation parlance is 'nothing to do with the distance between two points'.

Unconscious humour is often present when someone describes some unusual aviation experience. Jokingly referred to as a 'Line' or 'line shoot' it is quickly forgotten if not written down at the time. We are therefore very fortunate that Tony Hobson not only still has the 50 year old battered line book in which he recorded 'lines' from his days as a flying instructor in South Africa, but also the outstanding original drawings he created at the time to illustrate those lines. The originals are faithfully reproduced in this book in a way which will bring many a smile to the faces of those who have the slightest interest in aviation.

Ivor Broom

1995

xi

AUTHOR'S COMMENT

Jorrocks said about hunting that it was 'the himage of war without the guilt, and only five-and-twenty per cent of the danger', and the same sentiment could be applied to Service flying instruction. Behind the excitement of that release into the upper atmosphere there lie a hundred small concerns for the safety of aircraft and pupils, the routine of form-filling, the occasional boredom and frustration of ex-operational pilots, the daily life of the Mess: and yet, when all is said and done, who would not fly if he could?

Although accompanied by some descriptive notes, mainly about aircraft which may not be familiar to the present-day reader, this is not a nostalgic memoir but fundamentally a war-time view of flying training. The lines were all shot and the author's drawings were all done at the time, in the Air Schools in which he served; they crackle with the humour of immediate observation among young men undergoing the greatest experience of all – that of taking a ton of metal into the sky and making it answer to man's will. The rewards of the flying instructor are balanced, almost always light-heartedly, against that most difficult of all human tasks: getting the other chap to do what you think he ought!

Ilmington
October 1995

ABOUT THE AUTHOR

Tony Hobson left school to study at Leicester College of Art, and in 1939 applied to join the RAF Volunteer Reserve as a pilot. However, having informed the Air Commodore that there were forty-five degrees in a right angle, this project was deferred until after his call-up as a Clerk/Clerk Accounts, when he persisted with his aircrew applications. In due course these bore fruit, and after a further board which revealed that the interviewing officer and his assistant did not themselves know the capital of Australia and where Tony astounded the medical officers by performing a half-arm planche on the edge of a table, he left No. 1 RAF Depot, Uxbridge, and his Morgan three-wheeler via PRC Bournemouth for 17 ITW Scarborough, where during a bottleneck in training he painted some fine aircraft murals on the walls of that recently evacuated girls' boarding school.

Selected at last for pilot training, he was kitted out with khaki and pith helmet and embarked for South Africa under the Empire Air Training Scheme. South African Air Force instructors both pleasant and unpleasant contrived to bring him up to Wings standard; he was awarded the RAF Flying Badge on 18th February 1944, commissioned and posted to the Central Flying School at Bloemfontein to become a flying instructor. Eighteen months instruction at Bloemspruit and Vereeniging, where complete harmony existed between RAF and SAAF, brought his flying hours over the 1000 mark, mostly on Harvards. After his release in 1945 and promotion to Flight Lieutenant, he flew for a further six years with the RAF Volunteer Reserve on Tiger Moths and Prentices – promised Chipmunks but they never came!

Never without pencil, pen and colours, the South African years saw the birth of the 'C' Flight Line Book, and back in England he rejoined the College of Art and qualified with Diplomas in Painting and Art Teaching while owning two more Morgans. Painting continuously, he was nevertheless drawn to the study of art history, and while a Polytechnic Head of Department was awarded the degree of Doctor of Philosophy for his thesis on the Victorian painter J. W. Waterhouse, RA, which was followed by two best-selling books. Now an Honorary Research Fellow of Coventry University, he is in demand as a lecturer – both independently and teaching regular courses for Warwick University – and as a painter of ceremonial portraits including the life-size series of Provincial Grand

Masters at Edgbaston, Birmingham, and of celebrated players in the Tennis Court at Lord's. Still life, figure paintings and of course aircraft subjects like those illustrated here are still within his area of operation. He has exhibited with the Society of Aviation Artists as well as at the Royal Academy, the Royal Scottish Academy and all the major Royal Societies such as the Portrait Painters. During the intervening years he has lectured in Canada and the United States, travelled round Australia on a lecture tour, and returned to South Africa for an Air Force Reunion.

It was the laughter heard in the Mess, the heaven-sent gift of ludicrous exaggeration, and the graphic phrases born of close personal encounters, which gave rise to 'shooting a line' in the Royal Air Force. This was a habit as common in the Air Schools as on the operational squadrons, and the 'lines' in this book will find a response somewhere in the heart of every Service pilot, wherever he trained. The author was fortunate, as a member of the team of 'C' Flight flying instructors at 27 AS Bloemspruit, in being on hand to illustrate the aphorisms which flowed so freely from that happy company under the aegis of the Flight Commander, Captain Tony Lawrenson, SAAF. Both these officers were posted in due course to 22 AS Vereeniging, where a second burst of lines took place.

The drawings culled from that battered exercise book, the 'C' Flight Line Book, were done in the intervals of flying, mostly in the year of Our Lord 1944. The single-engined aircraft featured throughout is the famous North American Harvard Mk.IIA, on which many thousands of RAF and SAAF pupils gained their wings.

As the line-shooters were all positively identified on the spot and the lines documented by reliable witnesses, no attempt has been made to disguise their names. They appear word for word – and face for face! – as they did at the time. It is heartening to look back and realise that if in some sense there was little privacy in such a company, neither was there anything put down which exceeded the bounds of broad good humour and fellow-feeling. It has only been necessary, for the benefit of the reader, to attempt some sort of grouping of the lines which flowed so thick and fast on a variety of subjects.

INTRODUCTION

The Empire Training Scheme was devised in order to provide clear skies in which pilots could learn to fly, and navigators to navigate, without being shot down by marauding enemy aircraft. Cadets were sent for training to Canada, to South Africa and Rhodesia, and by courtesy to America. Oddly enough, there were those who on arrival, although perfectly fit in the normal sense, proved unable to land the aircraft with safety. Theirs was therefore a wasted journey, and led to the establishment in Britain of the Grading School, where young men could prove by a solo flight within twelve hours of instruction that they possessed the physical coordination to warrant an overseas posting for further training up to Wings standard.

The cordial reception of RAF cadets overseas was much the same everywhere. In South Africa they were taken to the hearts of families whose sons were fighting in the Western Desert alongside British troops – 'up North', as they said. Queues of cars formed at the airfield gates to offer hospitality to the RAF, and the author was only one of many hundreds of cadets who found a second home with a South African family. They served side by side in equal numbers with South African Air Force personnel, and the same applied to those selected and retained as flying instructors. Of the latter, there were many aircrew, both RAF and SAAF, posted back to instructors' duties after flying operations in the Desert, and there were also RAF pilots who arrived after flying in the Battle of Britain. All had been in the thick of the struggle against the Axis powers, and many had wounds and decorations to show for it: the same applied to the soldiers whom we met on leave, and who in common with the airmen are now among the 'senior citizens' of South Africa. We are still in their debt, as indeed to all the South African troops who volunteered to fight not only in North Africa but in Italy and elsewhere beyond the call of duty and their nominal obligations, and won six Victoria Crosses and left a thousand dead in our cause.

At the Air Schools, the atmosphere was a kind of light-hearted intensity within the disciplines and procedures of air safety and comprehensive instruction: the Wartime Air Training Scheme in Southern Africa alone trained over 30,000 pilots and navigators for active service. Detached from the theatres of war solely in order to take advantage of clear skies in which training could be carried on uninterrupted, there were still the normal hazards of flying to be encountered, together with the sometimes unpredictable behaviour of the pupil pilot in the flush of trepidation, enthusiasm or disastrous over-confidence. Even experienced instructors occasionally felt the adrenalin flowing more swiftly in the intoxicating freedom of flight, but they generally sobered quickly at the dangers of low-flying practice, or night landings prior to the pupil's first solo, or the fortunately rare occurrence of the nervous pupil who had a mental blackout and 'froze' on to the controls during a spin.

"Platinum playthings"? – "Chromium-plated spam-cans"? – only joking!
The North American Harvard Mk.IIa, uncamouflaged in South African skies.

At 22 Air School, Vereeniging; based on an early Ford chassis, the extraordinary but efficient Hucks starter, which engaged and rotated the Hart propeller in the absence of the hand-cranked inertia starter.

It was named after the inventor, Bentfield C. Hucks (1884–1918), one of the greatest pioneer flyers, test pilot, Royal Flying Corps, and the first Englishman to loop the loop and fly upside down. He gave sensational trick flying displays in 1914, using a Bleriot monoplane with a 60 h.p. Gnome engine and rings painted on the wings, which fore-shadowed the standard Service markings but were then intended simply to enable spectators to gauge the changing attitudes of the aircraft.

THE PERILS OF PILOTING

Is it significant that the Service Flying Log Book D.D. 461 provided four full pages headed 'Record of Flying Accidents' (with columns for 'Date', 'Cause' and 'Assessment of Blame') and only one page each for the pilot's 'Record of Service' and 'Aircraft Flown'? Fortunately, in the author's case the first four pages remained blank, but not all flying instructors were so lucky. There have always been flying accidents in the course of training, and by 1944 fewer airmen walked away from them than in the earlier days of slower (and more fragile) aircraft, although the Tiger Moth could always be relied upon to set its occupants down as gently as possible.

Nevertheless, it was the apprehension born of experience which saved many a life and limb: that, and the luck which attends both careful and foolhardy alike. How many pilots can look back on the moments which *might* have preceded disaster, but didn't: the lack of attention leading to a near miss or a stall; the sight of that awfully motionless airscrew as the engine stopped on top of a loop, on a misty day with no field in sight? But the possibilities always seem to have exceeded the actualities, and the characteristics of different aircraft became legendary warnings and in the end an aid to safety.

Some random RAF (and WAAF) types

APPREHENSIONS OF INSTRUCTORS

If it is true that the major characteristic of the pupil pilot was a cheerful insouciance born of total inexperience and a confidence that everything was going to be all right, the instructor was frequently plagued with a streak of doubt and the awareness that nasty things could happen if he failed to keep his finger on the pulse of events. The spontaneous reaction could well find its way into the Line Book, even though it might be impossible to illustrate: witness Lt Ashington – 'The pupil nearly killed me! – first time in my life I've ever used bad language.'

There were close calls giving rise to a rush of adrenalin, enhanced by the dual responsibility for keeping a sharp look-out.

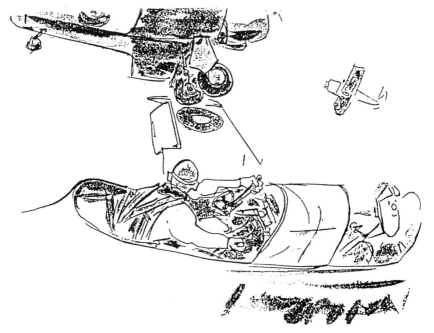

Capt Lawrenson:
'In a moment of panic I opened the 'throt' so fast that I bent the throttle quadrant.'

But the apprehension passed, once back on the ground. Capt MacLean was heard to say: 'I didn't even feel frightened today. I think I'll do some more flying.' This innate desire to risk one's life recalled for the artist a fellow-instructor who claimed:

'When I was a pupil I used to fly inverted through hangars.'

Some professed to having avoided taking the air.

Lt Condon:

'You can see when I last did any instruction. I shout for a pupil and then start coughing.'

More flying was in fact obligatory, and he afterwards came into line, saying:

'I do so much flying in C Flight, every time I get back on the ground my legs feel strange.'

(The ears were a feature)

Unauthorised low flying resulted in 45 pilots and pupils being killed between September 1941 and March 1944, as well as 14 seriously injured and 31 aircraft destroyed or damaged. The memorial outside Johannesburg, which incorporates a pair of Harvard wings, commemorates these and many more killed in training.

So some were still cautious after recent 'prangs'.

Lt Kelly:

'I do low flying nowadays with oxygen equipment.'

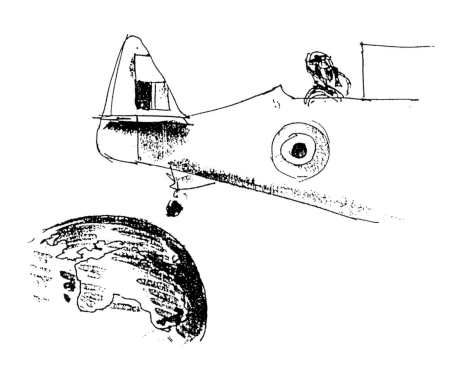

However, the fascination of low flying remained and the stories were still rife.

Major Blyth:
'One of the Pietersburg Oxfords came back from low flying with a pitchfork stuck in it.'

Pietersburg in the Transvaal was the home of 26 Air School, established in March 1942 with Miles Masters at an airfield in use since 1940 as an SFTS (Service Flying Training School, using Service aircraft, as distinct from the Elementary FTS with its Tiger Moths).

The Airspeed Oxford, based on the earlier Envoy, was a twin-engined training aircraft with side-by-side seating and a properly planned cockpit layout. Of the 8,586 actually built, 666 arrived in South Africa. It was (quite properly as a trainer) not an easy aircraft to fly well, but those who mastered it were well prepared for flying more powerful aircraft.

Natural disasters, of course, were things which could not be avoided, and one took every precaution.

S/Ldr Mason, hurling himself to the ground during a violent thunderstorm:
'Well, I'm earthed, anyway!'

Sgt Macduff complained about the difficulty of getting a homing on night cross-country exercises when there were so many aircraft radioing in for the same purpose.

By day, the low-flying cross-country was much more fun, and there was even a touch of bravado.

F/O Hedley:
"I was so low I had a stone thrown at me."

One simple true story will suffice to conclude the apprehension of instructors. The instructor concerned, a cheerful and (it must be said) efficient young officer, was teaching the recovery from a spin. They climbed to three thousand feet and put the aircraft into a spin – throttle back, stick back, full right rudder – and down they went vertically with the ground apparently revolving around the aeroplane. 'Recover!' said the instructor, and the pupil did the right things; stick forward, opposite rudder, stopping the spin, and eased the stick back to bring the plane out of the dive. They climbed again and repeated the exercise without incident. On the third occasion, however, when the instructor called 'Recover!' absolutely nothing happened: the pupil had suffered the not uncommon mental blackout and frozen on to the controls. This was something to be feared: the control column was totally immovable, the rudder bar likewise. The instructor was powerless. 'Recover! Recover!' he called twice more; but no response.

By this time the ground was coming up at an alarming rate. The theory was clear; under no circumstances abandon the aircraft with the pupil still in it. In practice, that was by no means an easy decision; should two lives be sacrificed or one? To cut a long story short, the instructor, having exerted all his efforts both vocal and physical to deal with the situation, gave his final order: 'Bale out! Bale out!' and, after delaying until the very last minute, did so himself.

The remainder of the story has to be comic rather than tragic. In the Harvard, as you will see, the instructor sits at the back; the canopy over him slides forward to open. As he opened the canopy, the rush of air through the cockpit woke the pupil up. The instructor, baling out, slid back along the fuselage, struck his head on the tailplane and came to in the air, floating down under his parachute, and rather badly bruised around his own fuselage through having had the parachute harness too loose.

The pupil, seeing the ground looming up, brought the aircraft out of the spin with all despatch and, possibly aggrieved at having (as he thought) had no orders to do so, turned round to see behind him an empty cockpit with the straps flying in all directions. Understandably panicking, he put the aircraft nose down again and headed for the airfield, somehow landed safely and taxied madly for the flight office, where he leapt out, leaving the plane still rolling across the tarmac. Observing this from his office window, the flight commander, a distinguished ex-operational pilot with an unfortunate stammer in addition to his DFC, charged out to meet him. What they stammered to each other is not recorded, but the instructor, who had parachuted down a couple of miles away, was taken off flying – and went on living. No drawings were made.

Crashed Hawker Hind, showing the propeller boss.

A 'Hart to Hart' encounter.

AIRCRAFT AND AIRFIELDS

Some instructors felt that pride in the appearance of the aircraft could be overdone. *P/O Sweetman*:

'Our kites are so heavily painted they'll never get off the deck.'

However, it was their flying condition which was of prime concern. The aircraft illustrated here is the North American Harvard Mk.IIA, which was very well liked. It was reliable and good for training, being somewhat demanding to fly accurately but very positive in accustomed hands. Fast wheel landings, as opposed to three-pointers, and using the full length of the airfield, became a pleasant diversion for the slightly bored instructor, and the mighty downward plunge of the Pratt & Whitney radial engine after the Harvard reared up into a stall is not to be forgotten. Visually, it differed from the Mk.I's curves in having clipped wingtips and an angular fin and rudder, and from the artist's point of view its unmistakable outline was very satisfying to draw.

As supplies of alloy increased, earlier fabric (in the Mk.I) and plywood fuselages gave way to an all-metal structure which survived South African conditions so well that deliveries eventually outpaced requirements, and brand-new Harvards were put into store. The final triumph of the Harvard was its continued use as a basic trainer after an unsuccessful experiment with all-through jet training, and today something like a hundred of them can be seen on the SAAF Central Flying School tarmac.

The Miles Master, used before the introduction of the Harvard, was not a success in African conditions. Although fast and manoeuvrable, it had a sensitive engine – the Bristol Mercury II – unsuited to ham-fisted handling by pupils. Due to technical problems and a number of fatal and non-fatal crashes, only about one-third of them were serviceable at any one time, and at one period lines of drooping Masters might be seen on the airfields, their wooden airframes having been eaten by termites.

Flt/Lt Rutherford:

'Serviceability was so bad on the Masters that we flew the boxes they came in.'

Also present were a few Hawker Hart variants, used for the morning 'met' flight due to their altitude capability. (See photographs) The observer took readings from instruments on the interplane struts.

Occasionally other aircraft came visiting. A couple of Lockheed Venturas turned up, with a certain reputation for being difficult to fly, eliciting remarks like: 'These Venturas are disappointing; no one has pranged yet.'

They were of course flown by experienced pilots like *Capt Angus-MacLean*, who imparted his knowledge of them to the rest of us:

'Warning of the stall in a Ventura is given by juddering of the controls – and a scream from MacLean.'

The Ventura, similar in shape to the Hudson, was a military development of the Lodestar transport produced to meet a British contract placed in the summer of 1940. Its long range was acquired through a rather complicated fuel system and large fuel tanks·

Lt Cuckow:
'A Ventura is a petrol tank with two wingtips.'

Concrete runways were largely a thing of the future, and the grass airfield was subject to the vagaries of the weather.

Major Dennett (inspecting the aerodrome after several inches of rain have fallen):
'It's not too wet: there's still dust blowing off it.'

13

Nor was the equipment of the auxiliary airfield above suspicion.

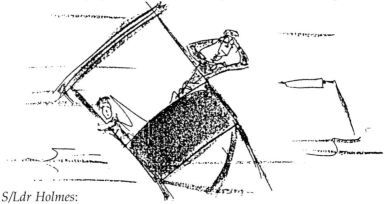

S/Ldr Holmes:
'The watch tower at Blydschap sways 30° in a high wind.'
However, senior officers were anxious to establish their reputation for supervising these facilities.

S/Ldr Mason:
'I was on the aerodrome at six o'clock this morning.'
We understand that this relates to an actual incident (*not* concerning this particular officer).

In some, the primitive conditions evoked operational memories.

Lt Boutell:
'I like being Safety Officer on the bombing range; it makes me think I'm back in the Desert.'

Which recalls *Major Dennett*, describing raids in a Boston:

'The flak was so intense, we lowered the wheels and taxied over it.'

Miles Master after a bad landing.

Air Chief Marshal Sir Arthur Tedder visiting No. 22 Air School, Vereeniging, to present wings to pupil pilots. With him, Air Vice-Marshal M.B. Frew, AOC Training Command, and Group Captain J.F. Roulston. 'Bunty' Frew transferred to the RFC in 1916 from the Highland Light Infantry and won the DSO after shooting down three enemy aircraft in a single combat and gliding five miles to the Allied lines with his engine out of action. In 1931–32 he won a bar to his DSO in Kurdistan, together with the MC, AFC and the Italian Silver Medal for Military Valour.

AGE AND EXPERIENCE

Instructors were of course at pains to emphasise their long experience of flying.

Flt/Lt Rutherford:
'This wind is even dangerous for me to fly in.'

Even the most recent promotion imparted a feeling of superiority.

F/O Hedley:
'I have an aircraft test to do and I'm an *F/O*; with all these sprogs in my section, too!' ('Sprog' = a junior, inexperienced; in this case referring to fellow instructors still Pilot Officers.)

And *Rutherford* again:

'When I did my training there weren't any gliders.'

Even small items of dress could reinforce the desired impression.

Capt Lawrenson:
   'I don't have to tell people how much experience I've got. They've just got to look at my cap.'

And Lawrenson went on to say, after Lt Ashington said *he* was beginning to feel ashamed of his small monthly flying hours:

'I'm never ashamed of my total, no matter how small, because *one* of my hours is worth *twenty* of anyone else's.'

Though *Lt Allen* was heard to say of another pilot, with guarded admiration:

'That chap's been an instructor a hell of a time. He was even an instructor when *I* was a pupil.'

Major Dennett was quoted as saying:

'Before Waterkloof was a station, it was a forced landing ground,'

evoking the suggestion that presumably before that it was a Roman camp.

19

Waterkloof, where the author gained his Wings, has indeed an impressive history. Still a major Air Force base, it celebrated its 50th anniversary in 1988.

Rather more specifically, *S/Ldr McKnight* said:

'When the Rhodesian Air Training Scheme first started, I once saw a lion chasing a Harvard around the aerodrome.'

Air Chief Marshal Sir Arthur Tedder (as he was then) taking the salute at the passing-out parade.

Large Harvard formation at Air Display, Newmarket Race Course, Johannesburg. The author is on the right.

THE PUPIL PILOT

The pupil pilot was of course the reason for the Air Schools – and vice versa. Pre-War, pilot training in South Africa had been shared between flying clubs and SAAF units which provided advanced instruction, but after a succession of agreements instigated by General Smuts the Joint Air Training Scheme covering both SAAF and RAF was formally initiated in June 1941. By 1943, the RAF cadets were being supplemented by some other nationalities such as Greeks, Poles and Yugoslavs. Their numbers were not great, but at Waterkloof, the author remembers particularly the two Belgian cousins Eid coming from Egypt, with superb uniforms which made our RAF khaki look extremely drab!

The sheer number of pupils (some 30,000 in all) made generalisations risky, but certain opinions were understandably common among instructors.

Capt Lawrenson:
'With the aid of the Handling Notes, a low intelligence ape could solo in twelve hours.'

Would that all pupils had followed suit! But in spite of the Grading School experience, a few were still liable to be 'washed out'. At one end of the scale, there was an incompetence born perhaps of timidity, while at the other, a danger was certainly the over-confidence bred of a few hours at the controls.

F/O Homes:
'That bloody pupil thinks he is Baron Richthofen.'

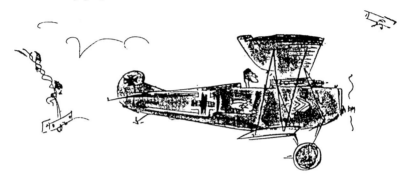

Pilots of the 1940s were still steeped in the memories of 1914–18, and the name of the 'Red Baron' has survived even into the age of Snoopy. Baron Manfred von Richthofen, the highest scoring German ace, gained most of his eighty victories in a Fokker triplane, but the artist here took the liberty of showing him in the earlier Fokker D.VII – himself repeating one of the many drawings he made of this and other aircraft of the Great War as a boy of fifteen. Richthofen was a disciplined fighter, by no means exhibiting the reckless confidence implied in P/P Matthews; he had little use for stunts, and boasted that he had never looped the loop nor ever intended to do so.

A sensitive touch on the controls was not easily acquired. Ham-fisted *over*-correction could be the order of the day – and a strain both on the aircraft and the instructor; witness *Sgt Macduff*:

'I've just been up on an air-sickness test: formation flying with P/P Byham.'

Bewilderment was certainly just around the corner, re-casting one of the oldest lines of all:

F/O Scotland:
'There was I, upside down, nothing on the clock, with the pupil taking astro sights through the bomb hatch . . .'
As *F/O Smith* was heard wryly to remark:

'These pupils are supposed to be the cream of England's youth – but by the time they reach South Africa they're a bit clotted.'
'Clot' = a stupid person (Concise Oxford Dictionary).

P/P Davies, when asked by P/O Homes what he did with the tail trim, replied:

'I push it forward and pull it back'!

Nevertheless, unlikely as it seemed at times, most of them managed to complete the course and take part in the Wings Parade – just as we had done; and they received the appropriate compliments.

Administrator Dr Barnard, addressing Pupil Pilots of 25 Course on receiving their wings:

'Today, you men are the shining light of freedom in the air.'

Rutherford, Sledmere, Hobson

OFF THE TARMAC AND INTO THE MESS

Fortunately, a normal life still went on away from the rigours of flying instruction. Of course, distractions were still desired. There were the local 'hops'.

After a dance at Tweespruit;
F/O Freer (admittedly not a tall man):
'She gave me a circuit and bump, after which I had DT's.'
And the Mess bar:
W/Cdr Alington (at 2130 hours):
'For the next half hour I shall fight a losing battle with the Demon Alcohol.'

And *Capt Jones*:
'Because of the meat shortage, I have to drink beer for its nutritive value.'

S/Ldr Holmes:
'I shall be glad when
I get married, as I needn't drink then.'

A wholesome remark: indeed, vast amounts of tea were drunk, particularly around the Flight office. If one could spare the time, the Tea Club could be a nice little sideline.

30

Lt Angus-Leppan was heard to say on the telephone:
'Ag, man, I'm *busy!*' –

Flt/Lt Rutherford:
'Since F/O Hedley took over the Tea Club, he has bought a new greatcoat, Angus-Leppan has new piston rings, and the two are off to the bioscope every night.' ('Bioscope' = that delightful South African synonym for the cinema.)

31

Whereas *Hedley* himself protested:

'I wish I could get rid of the Tea Club: I can't make ends meet.'

Well, savings had to be made. Another (and cheaper) form of transport was always welcome. Heard by the CO:

'I saw P/O Tawn and P/O Hobson on Saturday, going into town on their jallopy. I suppose the weekend is the only time they dare risk such a long trip.'

The familiar presence of our chaplain always served to divert and amuse.

Capt (Padre) Heath, accused of paying bridge debts with the collection money:

'That'll be the day when the collection is as much as the debts.'
and referred somewhat ruefully to

'the day when the CI does my job – the Conversion of Instructors.'
(One of the responsibilities of the Chief Instructor was converting pilots on to a new type of aircraft.)

He did, however, express his willingness to depart for the battle area if required:

'I'm fit to go up North. I've given up drinking and smoking.'
Some instructors (the Flight Commander among them) had domestic duties to occupy them.

Capt Lawrenson:
'I've trained my daughter well. There's no difficulty about getting her to sleep – I read L.M.U.42, 1732 B, and the M.D.C. to her and she soon drops off.'

Married officers were permitted to live off the base, and were thereby well equipped to deal with happenings laughingly said to be unexpected.

Lt O'Hara (after a happy event):
'I went home that night, and a little girl opened the door. I asked her who she was, but she answered 'Ssh, Mummy's sleeping'.'
F/O Smith:
'Dick O'Hara will be sorry the baby is a girl. It won't be able to grow a moustache.'

What other diversions were there?

F/O Freeman:
'The Station magazine is quite good – not as good as 'Esquire', though.'
These were the days before 'Playboy', when we were all innocents abroad, and the truly gorgeous girl drawn by Varga for the January 'Esquire' concealed her charms beneath her long hair and actually wore knickers.

Our extra-curricular injuries were suffered in games and sports.

Lt Cuckow:
'I strained a muscle in my groin yesterday. I was playing cricket.'

This in spite of being (as he claimed)

'the top scoring batsman of the Bloemfontein area.'

Feeble attempts were made to stop drinking.

Capt Clarke:
'I won't have a beer, thanks. I'll have a Lion Juice' (a mysterious concoction of South African origin).

Though this was faintly belied by other observations of this charming officer, such as:

'Do you mind if I catch the 5 o'clock bus? I told my wife I'd be home at 7.30.'

And the witness added:
'The shades of night were falling fast
As through the bar doors Nobby passed.'

Excuses were found, of course.

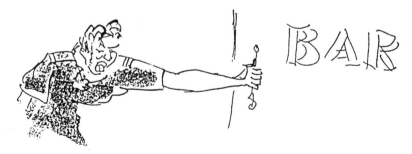

F/O Smith:
'The only reason I come into the bar is to get rid of the dust.'

And *Blackie Rutherford* had the best excuse of all for ceasing to imbibe
– the cash flow;

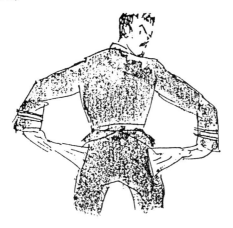

though as he put it:
'I've given up getting drunk now – there isn't any sense in it.'

Equestrian arts were practised, with varying degrees of success.

The CI:
'I can't ride a horse. It hasn't got a throttle.'

Of whom further testimony came.

Lt Col Pretorius:
'Only one man on this Station can do a 3-pointer: W/Cdr Alington, when riding a donkey.'

(The perfect three-point landing, now largely out of use with the advent of the tricycle undercarriage, was when the two main wheels and the single tail wheel all touched the ground simultaneously.)

Some, like *Major Dennett,* managed to avoid all unnecessary exertion, 'This afternoon I am doing Gyppo P.T. – flat on my back.'

However, it is pleasing to record that Jack Homes (he of the magnificent moustachios) was willing to enter every kind of sport.

S/Ldr Mason:

'At the water-polo match the other night, the spectators were throwing fish to F/O Homes.'

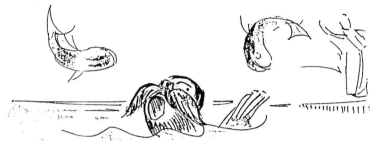

While at football – 'I only let two goals through in a whole season.'
Note: F/O Homes only played one game!

And as he said: 'I've paid in so much for billiards, I should be an honorary member of Thurston's.'

". . . Blacked out in the turn, so I switched on my cockpit lights . . ."

OVER THE TOP

Founded in the facts of flying, most 'lines' had a glimmer of truth; for instance,

F/O Smith:

'The breeze was so strong that when I stopped into wind my air speed indicator registered 40 mph.'

But thankfully a random selection proves that the true 'line' exceeds the bounds of credibility. Night flying in particular seems to have brought out a number of weird occurrences.

F/O Freer:

'The wind was so strong last night that it even blew the beam of the landing lamp around.'

And the CO:

'I don't know whether it's my magnetic personality, but I always generate static during a storm.'

Lt Boutell:
'It was so dark on the circuit I had to follow in the slipstream of the aircraft in front of me.'

Obviously, this was nothing to the darkness of the storm:

Lt Preston:
'When flying through a thunderstorm in formation this afternoon, Mundy-Castle flew so close that the lightning fused the two machines together.'

The late afternoon thunderstorm was a fact of life, common to the Transvaal. It was generally followed by a perfectly clear night for flying, when *F/O Smith* could claim:

'The moon was so strong I had to pull the I.F. hood over to prevent myself from getting moonstroke.'

The instrument flying hood was a standard piece of equipment fitted in the rear cockpit to enable the pupil to practise flying solely by instruments, the instructor being in the front seat for a change, with the better view.

Nearer the ground, however, things were less clear.

F/O Smith again:

'There was so much dust on the flarepath tonight, I couldn't get the airscrew in coarse.'

(For today's jet-propelled public, this rather technical line refers to the purely mechanical business of adjusting the pitch of the airscrew from coarse to fine – a sort of gear-changing to assist in take-off.)

45

Formation flying was a test of skill and aircraft handling, and its problems were unlikely to be overcome by *P/O Tawn*:
'I kept overshooting in formation, so I applied my brakes.'

Fun was clearly more fun when done in formation.

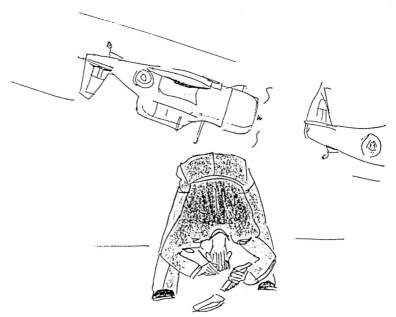

Major Blyth:
'The last shoot-up we did in line astern, the leader was so low that the fellow at the back flew upside down so that his number couldn't be taken.'

That challenging and not wholly original remark, 'I've flown more types than you have hours' (P/O Farley to P/O Hobson) was improved upon by *Lt Ashington*:

'I've got more hours over the cone of silence . . .' (the brief cessation of audible blips in the Beam Approach system when over the target, simulated here by Ashington in the hooded Link Trainer.)

There were, it must be admitted, one or two differences of opinion, or simply affectations of disbelief, such as when

Lt "Kittyhawk" Denny (challenged about the signed letter his family received from Winston Churchill) roared:
'At my home, we've got enough personal letters from Winston Churchill to use on a ******* pamphlet raid!'

Or in rejoinder to P/O Farley (who really *had* fought in the Battle of Britain, as a Sergeant Pilot), *P/O Dyson* averred:

'The Battle of Britain was won by George Farley and Air Marshal Dowding. Dowding signed the Authorisation Book' – the book in which every flight had to be authorised by the Flight Commander or other senior officer.

Sometimes, of course, it was sheer bravado which evoked the line.

Lt Cuckow:
'When I was posted here, two hundred men were posted away.'

Sometimes a slip of the tongue produced the unlikely result.

P/O Sweetman (in the course of conversation):
'... I did a normal 90°-banked turn ...'
And perhaps grounds for a medical discharge were being sought?

Lt Boutell:
'I have disproved Einstein's theories. I can see you when I am round the bend.'

A recent oil painting by Tony Hobson:
"Harvards Homing – Storm Gathering"

"C" FLIGHT SUPREME

So there we are. All roads seemed to lead to 'C' Flight.

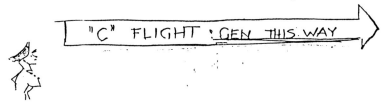

Capt Jones:
'I wanted some 'gen', so I came to 'C' Flight, of course.'
We had splendid examples from high up;
Brigadier Daniels:
'Instruction? I loved it to death.'

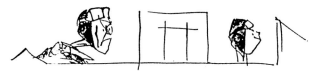

and a high moral tone;
Capt Lawrenson:
'I was kept so pure and untainted when I was young that the stories told in the Flight don't mean a thing to me.'

He combined this with great powers of leadership:

Capt Lawrenson:
'Another two drinks and I'll revolutionise the station this afternoon.'
(N.B. F/O Homes is away on sick leave)

'C' Flight efficiency was obvious – especially to 'C' Flight personnel.
Lt Ashington:
'You can set your watch by the hum of our aircraft as they take off at 0700 hours.'

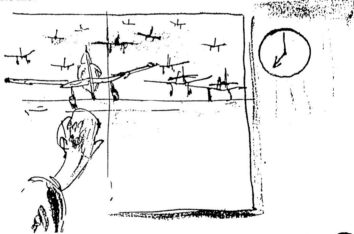

A keen eye was kept upon any irregularities.
Capt Orr (after booking 30 minutes flying as one hour):
'Well, I had to fly at 2100 revs all the time.'

Comparisons were inevitable.

Capt Lawrenson:
'After looking across the aerodrome at a 'prang', I knew it wasn't one of *my* aircraft – it wasn't clean enough.'

Not that one wished to knock the opposition, but –

Capt Lawrenson again:
'You chaps had better say good-bye to me. I'm going to fly a 'D' Flight machine.'

Was there indeed a touch of envy at the confident acceptance of possible hazards?

Capt Lawrenson (when P/P Aske was calling for QDMs):
'Oh, he's probably flown into a stuffed cloud.'

Or was it merely that, as *Capt Evan-Jones* stated:
'A line is nothing to do with the distance between two points: it's something you find in 'C' Flight.'

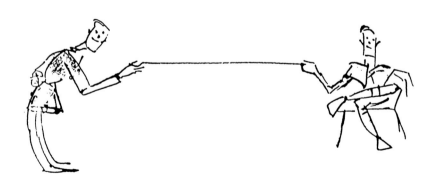

Or perhaps it was just sheer admiration at 'C' Flight versatility and all-round brilliance.

F/O Scotland, heard in the Mess bar:
'I want to buy a copy of 'C' Flight magazine.'

"I learnt all about AIRFRAMES at E.F.T.S."

WHAT'S IN AN APPENDIX?

In due course, Capt Lawrenson was posted to command No. 1 Group at 22 Air School, Vereeniging, in the Transvaal. The flow of lines continued there unabated, and as the author had accompanied Tony Lawrenson on this posting a number of fresh characters appeared in the new One Group Line Book, led (as it happened) by *F/O Bailes* (never accused of being over-modest), declaiming:

'I'm so split-arse the ball keeps its eye on me.'
('Split-arse' = an expression now perhaps permissible in print; of obscure origin, but meaning incredibly skilled and precise in action.)

Bailes it was who was heard to say to the flight commander, after his pupil had done only two hours on the Harvard:

'Sir, can you take my pupil on a Passenger Test?' – a test which could qualify the pilot not merely to go solo, but to take a non-qualified passenger.

The instructor is seen here, blindfolded and waving the (detachable) control column as evidence of his confidence in the pupil – and in his own teaching.

Also wielding the 'stick', in another context, is one of those referred to by *Capt Klopper*, when he said:

'Pilots are always good-tempered.'

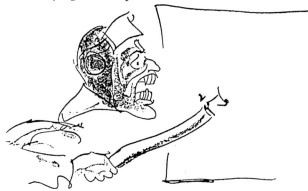

A delightful character was *F/O Gordon-Cumming* (we were all F/Os by this time), who kept a parrot in his room and transported it in a Harvard on his next posting. He was heard to say more than once:

'I don't know how you fellows get on without a parrot.' He too affected a remarkable precision in flying, with this observation intended for the technically-minded:

'I came in to do my normal three-pointer (see page 40), but as the main wheels touched first, I knew the tail oleo was flat.'

The Harvard tail wheel was mounted on a resilient oil-filled leg. An entry in the F.700 recorded 'Tail oleo has no give', and the response, under 'Placed Serviceable', read 'Tail oleo given some give'.

The three-point landing was always the ideal, and one can imagine the aircraft itself straining to assist.

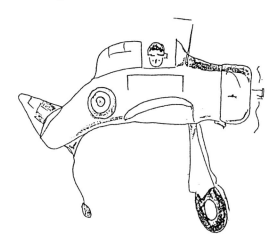

Lt Miles (more in hope than in fact?):
'You always know my pupils by their three-point landings.'

Truly was it said by *Lt Van Rooyen*:
'The man who designed the Harvard undercarriage should get the CBE.'

Major Theron testified to the stresses and strains on the undercart:
'I believe P/P Booth stutters a lot – and he stutters in his landings, too!'

The third component of the undercarriage was of course the tail wheel or tail skid. Tail skids on the early Harts and Tiger Moths tore up the grass airfields and were not particularly efficient in directing the aircraft along a chosen path; most pilots will be familiar with the spectacle of a Tiger Moth in a high wind, revolving on its axis in the middle of the aerodrome until a pair of helpers arrive and steer it home by the wingtips. Tailwheels succeeded in lessening the resulting dust, which not only reduced visibility but was drawn into the engines: however, they were not always coupled to the rudder, which could still make steering difficult.

Lt Miles was not to be deterred:
'Certainly I'll fly an aircraft with an uncoupled tailwheel. I've been flying aircraft with unserviceable and fully castoring tailwheels for years.'

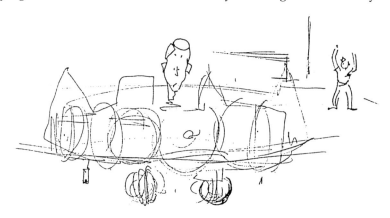

Miles, a former Desert pilot, could exhibit a remarkable *sang-froid*:

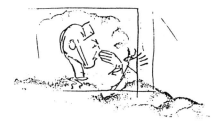

'I thought I could smell burning oil, so I closed the canopy.'

Some hazards were apparently unavoidable. *F/O Gordon-Cumming*:

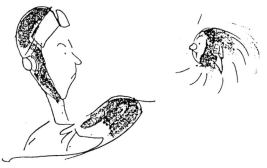

'When they were testing the signal mortar recently, I nearly got shot down.'

And some were not. *Gordon-Cumming* complained:

'This pupil can't operate the parking brake. When I got out, the aircraft made a hungry run at Denis Quin.'

While *Lt Quin*, after nearly landing on Lt Van Rooyen, said:

'You fellows needn't worry when Quin is in the cockpit.'
Quin was tall, elegant and fairly imperturbable. He was also extremely slim, and not afraid to confess:

'When I have a shower, I have to move around to get the drops to fall on me.'

Or to claim:

'There was so much gravity in the turn, my eyeballs were forced down into my overall pockets.'

But others had to get a word in, generally about the pupils -although instructors could not escape. *Capt Davey* was heard to say:

'I can't send P/P Bowen with P/O Stansfield. It'll be worse than two drunken Dutchmen on a Harley-Davidson!'

Perhaps it was not surprising that *Quin* complained:
'I can't open my mouth without being slammed in the Line Book.'

Of course, the machine could always be blamed. *Lt Gibson*, arriving at the tarmac with his flaps still down:

'I wondered why the aircraft wouldn't taxi any faster!'
Flaps were of course normally used to slow the aircraft down when landing, although a harmless diversion of many instructors was the flapless 'wheel landing' at some 130 knots, which could take up most of the airfield. This was a delicate exercise in contrast to the three-pointer, with the aircraft running in on the main wheels and only being allowed to subside on to the tail-wheel at the last minute: an unwary foot on the brake could result in a cartwheel!

We could take 'em or leave 'em. *Capt Lawrenson*:
'Wheel landings? I haven't done one for years.'

(Possibly an unintentional misreading on the part of the artist!)

Who could be unaware of the Klaxon which sounded at the final throttle-back if the undercart was still up? – although one recalls a nervous young pilot at 11 OTU belly-landing a Curtiss Kittyhawk with the sound of the horn reverberating all round the airfield.

Experienced senior officers were always mindful of the possibilities. Only joking, though, was *Major Hill* talking to Major Nicolson:

'Let us know what time you're taking off. We've got a ropey fire crew on this afternoon.'

Off duty, a touch of bravado was always present. *S/Ldr Wallis (on the telephone):*

'This is the C-in-C Game Reserve here;' and
(was this merely wishful thinking?):
  'I have been carrying out tests on the P.61 – the 'Black Widow'. She's very nice to handle and has a beautiful undercarriage.'

and (*Wallis* again):

'You don't know what I've got to go through on Thursday night!'
But we were more inclined to go along with the milder disclaimer:

'I play cards with religious people every night and haven't touched
beer since last Friday.'

With the fair sex, real charm would always carry the day.
Lt Stewart (a cocky, ebullient SAAF type) at a Mess Dance:

'Lady, do the roses in your garden grow as red as the roses in your cheeks?'

There were indeed louder voices on the station. *'Doc' Forbes* said:

'Pop Klopper is the noisiest beggar I know!'

But when the two of them were at the rugby match, *F/O Hampson* observed that 'nobody could hear the spectators.'

and *Major Nicolson* stated, after a Wings Parade:

'I could hear Major Murray at 9000 feet.'
Major Murray was a pilot of considerable experience, with a DFC to show for it. In response to the WAAF who asked 'Would you like the Vital Actions Drill pasted up on your wall?' he answered courteously 'No thanks; I know my vital actions now,'

and admitted:
'I only shoot lines to get my name in the Line Book.'

The instructors were all kept fully occupied;
F/O Hampson:
'I have been giving so much patter, I can't touch the hand mike – it's red hot!'

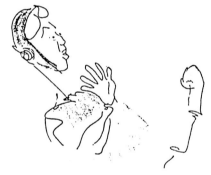

though there was a kind offer from the Engineer Officer, *Major Ridgers*:

'If we didn't have pilots, we'd fly the aircraft ourselves.'

But back to the pupil pilots – the reason for our existence. One sometimes wondered:
were some too tall for the job?
Said *F/O Gordon-Cumming*:
'P/P Penney's knees stick right out of the cockpit.'

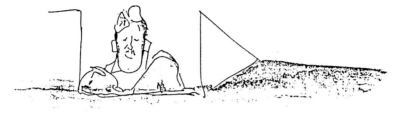

and *Lt Quin*:
'Send this pupil to the doc, to find out what keeps his ears apart.'

However, the pilot's cheerful nature overrode these minor inconveniences, shifting without difficulty to lighter things.

Lt Kannemeyer:
'I was listening to Bing Crosby on the radio, and I switched over to 'intercom' and carried on the song and the pupil didn't know the difference.'

And even the artist, unwary on one occasion, found himself too 'slammed in the Line Book'. *F/O Hobson:*
'I'm going on leave to Scottburgh – God's gift to South African women.'

Would it had been so! – or was it quite as bad as that?

But all good things came to an end, even the leave – and the Line Book.

Let *Capt Tony Lawrenson* have the last word, flying inverted as he says: 'I'm too tired to shoot lines these days.'

Here it is, then; large as life and twice as natural, as the old showmen used to say. The legend of 'C' Flight and 1 Group, with their personnel composed equally of red-tabbed khaki and RAF blue and commanded by Captain Tony Lawrenson, SAAF, is never going to fade. Old comrades who recognise themselves and others, pupils who identify their instructors – and young comrades who recognise their fathers – write in: perhaps we can add a few more pages!

TONY HOBSON

AND SOME MORE CARTOONS OF THE SAME VINTAGE

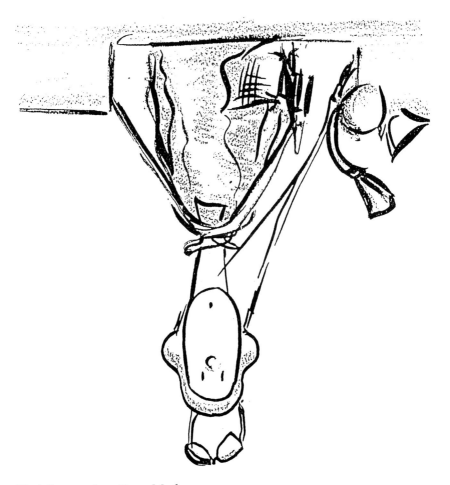

First time up in a Tiger Moth:-
    "Yes, sir, my straps are perfectly tight." Not so, I think!

"The Art of Instruction" (words actually spoken by flying instructors):

"As we approach the point of stall, the controls gradually fall off . . ."

"Now, place your feet lightly on the control column and your hands on the rudder bar . . ."

"But, sir, I'm sure I put red on red!" – a reference to the compass bearing.
(Had the instructor perhaps been asleep during this cross-country?)